There are eight different types of bear.

They all have large bodies covered with shaggy hair, stocky legs, long snouts, small rounded ears, and short tails. Their paws always have five claws.

Bears are good runners, climbers, and swimmers. They live in caves, and many hibernate in winter. They tend to live alone, except when they are cubs or have cubs.

While we often think of bears as soft and cuddly, they are in fact some of the most dangerous wild animals.

When polar bears stand up on their hind legs, they can be over ten feet tall (3m).

Bears hold onto the things that they are eating with their paws. They also use their paws to tug on leaves and bend trees so as to reach things higher up. They use their claws to dig, climb, tear, and catch things to eat.

bamboo

The claws on their forepaws are bigger than those on the back paws.

fresh salmon

Bears eat anything from leaves, roots, and berries, to insects, dead animals, fresh meat, and fish.

They have a very good sense of smell. They are very intelligent and can remember where they found food before.

The polar bear is the largest type of bear. They are found in the North, mainly in the Arctic circle. They have thick fur coats that protect them from the cold.

They have big paddle-like paws that are good for swimming, digging in the snow, and walking on ice.

They are excellent swimmers and can swim for days at a time.

They hunt seals, small walruses, and whales. They swim after these animals or wait next to ice holes and catch them when they come up to breathe.

Polar bear cubs are born while the mother is hibernating in a winter den under the snow. Female polar bears have two cubs at a time. The mother looks after and protects her cubs for two years or so after they are born.

The giant panda is possibly the most well known type of bear. It is instantly recognizable due to the black and white fur it is covered with.

Giant pandas mainly eat bamboo, and they have an extra finger on their paws that helps them to hold the bamboo canes.

When a giant panda baby is born, it is pink, hairless, and blind. It is interesting to note that under a panda's white fur, the skin is pink, but under the black fur, the skin is dark.

panda cubs

Giant pandas are endangered, as the places where they live, and where the bamboo grows, are vanishing. Pandas are only found in the wild in China, in six separate mountain ranges.

Despite their name, brown bears can be brown, black, or even blonde! They are also called grizzly bears. Brown bears are aggressive and sometimes attack people.

Brown bears mainly eat leaves, berries, roots, seeds, and nuts. They hibernate over the winter, living off the fat they have built up over the summer.

Male brown bears reach adult size at about eight years of age. They can live for up to 25 (twenty-five) years in the wild and over 40 (forty) years in a zoo.

The Himalayan black bear is sometimes called the moon bear. This is because they are covered with long, black fur and have a crescent-moon-shaped white patch on their chests.

Himalayan black bears eat small mammals, birds, fish, shellfish, and dead animals. They also eat berries, seeds, and insects. In autumn they fatten up for the winter by feeding on nuts.

Sun bears are the smallest type of bear. They have short black or dark brown fur, and a yellow crescent shape on their chests.

Sun bears have strong paws and no fur on the soles of their feet. They also have long, curved claws and flexible noses, or snouts, which are good for extracting termites from their nests.

The sloth bear has several teeth missing and uses this gap to suck up and feed on ants, termites, and other burrowing insects. They have large lips, a pale muzzle, or snout, and large hook-like claws that help them climb trees and dig for termites.

Sloth bears are nocturnal, so they only come out at night.

Sloth bears are stocky with long, shaggy, black hair, and they have a white U or Y shaped marking on their chests.

The spectacled or Andean bear is found only in the Andes mountains in South America. They are about five to six feet tall (1-2m). They can have jet black or dark brown fur.

They are called spectacled bears because they have light brown markings across their faces that look like spectacles. However, not every spectacled bear has "spectacles"!

Andean bears are also endangered in the wild due to loss of habitat (the places where they live).

The American black bear is the most common bear in America, and the smallest. They eat meat and vegetables, and live in forests, but can be tempted to leave the forest and approach people if they are looking for food.

black bear

Teddy bears are named after the American president Theodore, or "Teddy", Roosevelt. In 1902 he was on a bear hunting trip in Mississipi. As he hadn't yet shot a bear, someone tied a young black bear to a tree and suggested he should shoot it. Roosevelt refused to shoot the bear, saying that it was not fair.

an old teddy bear

A few days after that, a cartoon appeared in a newspaper showing Roosevelt refusing to shoot the bear. A shopkeeper called Morris Michtom saw the cartoon. His wife made a stuffed toy bear that they displayed in their shop called "Teddy's Bear," after President Roosevelt.

Theodore Roosevelt

We still call toy bears "teddy bears" today. To begin with, toy bears looked like real bears but now they come in all sorts of shapes and sizes. Someone who collects teddy bears is called an arctophile.

Magellan T Bear

In 1995, a teddy bear called Magellan T Bear went into space in a space shuttle!